CORNISH GARDENS

SALMON

INTRODUCTION

Blessed with a gentle climate and numerous great country estates, Cornwall is rich in superb gardens. Thanks to its situation in the far west of England, where it is warmed by the passing Gulf Stream and rarely suffers frost, Cornwall's climate is ideal for cultivating exotic species of trees and plants, many of them brought back to England by the great plant collectors of the Victorian era. Here dramatic sub-tropical jungles have been developed alongside ancient English woodland, formal gardens and sweeping lawns. From the county's most ancient estates such as Trelowarren, which has been in the hands of one family for 600 years, to the most recent creations such as the innovative Eden Project, established only in the 21st century, Cornwall provides endless stimulation for the keen plantsman and the weekend gardener alike. Here too there is relaxation and delight for anyone with an eye for the beauty of nature enhanced by the enthusiasm, skill and inspiration of generations of dedicated gardeners.

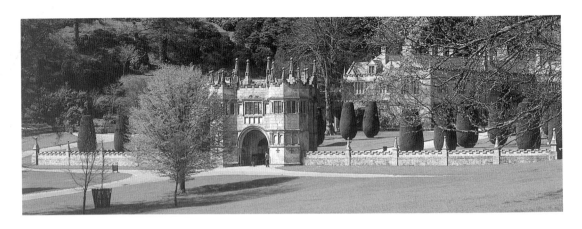

LANHYDROCK, near Bodmin

Overlooking the River Fowey to the south-east of Bodmin, Lanhydrock is superbly set in 450 acres of woodland and parkland planted with mature trees and rare shrubs which flourish in the mild climate. The Jacobean mansion was largely rebuilt in the 1880s following a fire, but the 17th century gatehouse still stands, surrounded by clipped yew trees. The formal gardens date from 1857 and are laid out with lawns and colourful flower-beds. The distinctive bronze urns which feature in the parterre garden were designed by Louis Ballin, goldsmith to King Louis XIV of France. Next to the house stands the little Church of St. Hydroc.

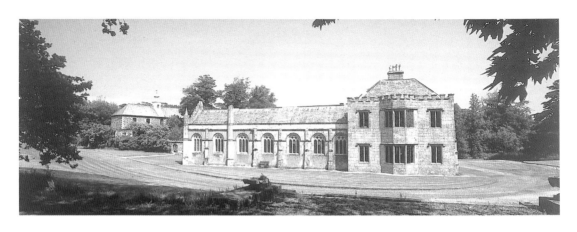

TRELOWARREN, Mawgan

One of Cornwall's most historic estates, Trelowarren has been in the continuous ownership of one family since 1427. Situated on the Lizard peninsula in the west of the county, the estate has won awards for its environmental projects which aim to make Trelowarren self-sufficient in food and energy, balancing the demands of a traditional working estate with conservation and the needs of wildlife. It is also home to the Cornwall Crafts Association, formed to support craftworkers living and working in the county. Another feature of the gardens is the existence of a series of underground chambers dating from Neolithic times.

TRELISSICK, Feock near Truro

The extensive gardens of Trelissick House, now owned by The National Trust, are favoured by the Gulf Stream and a warm, damp climate. They offer a tranquil atmosphere with a wonderful mixture of natural woodland and rare shrubs and plants including many varieties of azaleas, camellias and rhododendrons. In the shady wild garden, ferns, bamboos and other moisture-loving plants flourish while a definitive collection of Cornish apple varieties is being established in the orchard. There are extensive park, woodland and riverside walks, and the gardens offer panoramic views over the River Fal Estuary towards the open sea.

BONYTHON, near Helston

A major renovation of this splendid twenty-acre garden on the Lizard peninsula has been undertaken in recent years. Surrounded by the farm and woodland of the Bonython Estate, the sheltered gardens include formal planting, a walled garden, a herb garden and a potager. Added interest comes from the three lakes and an imaginative new planting scheme, much of it with an African theme including wild grasses, proteas, cannas and tree ferns. Planning for the future, more than fifteen thousand deciduous hardwoods have been planted to replace the original trees which are now more than two hundred years old.

ANTONY, Torpoint

Set in twenty-five acres of gardens and parkland landscaped by Humphry Repton, Antony is an outstanding 18th century house with lawns sweeping down to the River Tamar. Now owned by The National Trust, the gardens include a formal courtyard, terraces, an ornamental Japanese pond, fine summer borders and a knot garden. There are many species of native and exotic trees, and magnolias, azaleas, rhododendrons and camellias create a magnificent display in late spring. Additional interest is provided by stone carvings from India, a Burmese temple bell and William Pye's modern cone water sculpture on the west lawn.

TRENGWAINTON, near Penzance

Although there has been a house at Trengwainton for at least 500 years, the garden was largely created in the 20th century. Facing due south, it experiences a wonderfully mild climate which favours many species which are not grown in the open anywhere else in the country. It also has a magnificent collection of flowering shrubs, a walled garden and a woodland walk featuring an ornamental pond. The stream and bog garden have a charm of their own, planted with feathery bamboos, tree ferns, lilies, primulas and other water-loving plants. The Jubilee Garden, which was created in 1977, features New Zealand flax, agapanthus and lilies.

PENCARROW, near Bodmin

The gardens of Pencarrow, a splendid Palladian mansion situated near Bodmin, were created in the 1830s. A formal garden with a circular lawn is laid out on two sides of the house, but Pencarrow is particularly known for its fine woodland which includes specimen trees from across the world. Many of them line the mile-long carriage drive to the house together with flowering shrubs, primroses, daffodils and bluebells which make a colourful display in spring and early summer. A sunken Italian garden lies to the south of the house alongside the great rockery, which was built with blocks of granite carried from Bodmin Moor.

GLENDURGAN, Mawnan Smith near Falmouth

One of the great sub-tropical gardens of the south-west, Glendurgan occupies a steep-sided, wooded valley overlooking the Helford River. It is essentially a woodland garden with many specimen trees and conifers including two magnificent tulip trees which are nearly two hundred years old. It is a riot of colour in springtime with Lent lilies, bluebells, columbines and primroses growing in profusion, closely followed by a variety of flowering shrubs. The laurel maze, which dates from 1833, has been restored and there is also a fascinating "Holy Corner", planted with trees and shrubs which have Biblical associations.

TREVARNO, near Helston

One of the finest gardens in a county which is renowned for its great estates and gardens, Trevarno combines woodland areas with rare shrubs and trees, formal gardens and a lake with a cascade and a charming Victorian boat-house. The estate has been in existence since the late 13th century and a comprehensive and ongoing restoration programme during the last few years has made it possible once again to wander through restored Georgian and Victorian gardens, a wild flower garden, pinetum, serpentine yew tunnel and bluebell valley. Bygone gardening tools and implements are on display in a National Museum of Gardening.

EDEN PROJECT, St. Austell

Situated in an old claypit near St. Austell, the Eden Project is designed not only to display plants from around the world, but to protect endangered species and demonstrate the fascinating story of man's relationship with plants. Opened in 2001 and continuously improved and extended, it covers 125 acres and houses 4,000 species in giant domes which replicate the conditions in both tropical and temperate zones. The largest conservatory is 240 metres long by 55 metres high and is constructed from 800 huge steel hexagons. Enhanced by sculptures and an education centre, Eden has become one of the country's foremost tourist attractions.

TRERICE, near Newquay

Hidden away in a quiet valley, approached by a narrow, winding lane, Elizabethan Trerice Manor is known for its unusual and rare plants. Once, small enclosed gardens surrounded the house, which is owned by The National Trust, but today the aspect is more open. In front of the house colourful herbaceous planting leads down to lawns, while in the back court there are traditional cottage garden flowers including fuschias, honeysuckles and roses. The orchard is planted in the 17th century style and contains old varieties of apples, pears, quinces and plums. An interesting collection of historical lawn-mowers is housed in the barn.

GODOLPHIN, Helston

In the 17th century, Godolphin, situated some five miles from Helston, was the largest and grandest house in Cornwall, home of the Godolphin family who were prominent local landowners making their wealth from the tin-mining industry. Today only a part of the vast Tudor and Stuart estate remains, but this includes extensive gardens, farm buildings and the original Elizabethan stables. Some of the old formal gardens on the north and east sides of the house have been rediscovered, including a late medieval side garden. Complete with raised walks and carp ponds, they are currently undergoing clearance and restoration.

TREBAH, Mawnan Smith near Falmouth

First recorded in the Domesday Book in 1085, Trebah is built on a deep ravine which leads down to a sheltered cove on the Helford River. A stream cascades through the garden over waterfalls and ponds to the beach 200 feet below. The twenty-six-acre garden was begun in the 1840s but, like many Cornish gardens, it fell into neglect. Twenty-five years of restoration has now re-established a unique collection of rare and exotic plants offering year-round colour and scent. Ranging from sub-tropical Mediterranean plants to glades of tree ferns, bananas and bamboos from the rain forests, Trebah is a paradise for the plantsman and the artist.

MOUNT EDGCUMBE, Torpoint

Standing in an 865-acre country park on the Rame peninsula with magnificent views over Plymouth Sound, Mount Edgcumbe was described by Samuel Pepys, in 1683, as "the most beautiful place as ever was seen". Originally a wilderness garden, the present scheme was laid out in the 18th century. Italian and French gardens, overlooked by an orangery and a conservatory, contrast with the English garden, a pretty area with irregular lawns and some unusual trees including cork oak, ginkgo and paulownia. More recent additions are the American and New Zealand gardens, as well as a Jubilee garden, created in 2002.

MOUNT EDGCUMBE

COTEHELE, near Saltash

Enjoying a superb wooded situation high above the gorge of the River Tamar, Cotehele is now owned by The National Trust, but for many centuries it belonged to the Edgcumbe family who also lived at nearby Mount Edgcumbe. The gardens are on several levels with a formal terrace garden overlooking the Valley garden through which a little stream winds on its way to join the River Tamar. A medieval dovecote, a stewpond and a Victorian summer-house add interest to these delightful gardens which are known for their colourful flowering shrubs and trees including rhododendrons, azaleas, magnolias, maples and junipers.

HELIGAN, Pentewan near St. Austell

Lying forgotten and neglected for more than 70 years, the Lost Gardens of Heligan originated in the early 17th century. In an immense and ongoing feat of restoration, the largest garden restoration project in Europe, these unique and beautiful gardens are now being returned to their former splendour, providing a rare opportunity to observe the art of Georgian and Victorian gardening at its best. Among Heligan's many delights are walled gardens, lakes, an Italian garden and a "jungle" area extensively planted with bamboos, palms, tree ferns and other exotic plants which flourish in Cornwall's frost-free climate.

PENJERRICK, Budock near Falmouth

Created in the late 18th century by the Fox family, an old Falmouth Quaker family who also created gardens at Glendurgan and Trebah, Penjerrick is a garden of considerable historical and botanical interest. A relatively small, uncommercialised garden, it is known particularly for its rhododendrons, magnolias and camellias, but it also boasts a sub-tropical valley with ponds where bamboos and ancient tree ferns grow in a primeval setting. Among its many magnificent rare trees is the second largest beech tree in Britain. With many early-flowering plants and shrubs, this tranquil garden is at its best in spring.

TREWITHEN, Truro

Although the house and grounds at Trewithen date from the mid-18th century, the present-day gardens are largely the product of the last hundred years. Inheriting the estate in 1904, George Johnstone began a replanting scheme which has turned Trewithen into an internationally recognised garden, known for its beautiful and rare trees and shrubs, many of them found in very few other places in Britain. The formal gardens near the house complement the woodland areas with a sheltered walled garden enclosing a pond, a lawn edged with a wide variety of colourful shrubs and a pergola hung with wisteria.

INDEX

Printed and published by J. Salmon Ltd., 100 London Road, Sevenoaks, Kent TN13 1BB.
Telephone: 01732 452381   Email: enquiries@jsalmon.co.uk   Website: www.jsalmon.co.uk

ISBN 1 84640 031 7
Photographs by Chris Wormald

Pencarrow

Cotehele

Trerice

Lanhydrock

Eden Project

Antony

Mount Edgcumbe

Trewithen

Heligan

Trelissick

Trengwainton

Godolphin

Penjerrick

Trebah

Trevarno

Glendurgan

Bonython

Trelowarren